Butterflies, Dragonflies & Flowers
Adult Coloring Book

Butterflies, Dragonflies & Flowers
Copyright 2017 by Mabela Press
Developed by Kari Litscher
Images used under license from Shutterstock.com

All rights reserved. No portion of this book may be reproduced, stored in a retrieval system or transmitted in any form or by any means—electronic, mechanical, photocopy, recording, scanning or other—except for brief quotations in critical review or articles, without the prior written permission of the publisher.

Published in Oskaloosa, Iowa by Mabela Press. Mabela Press is an imprint of Mabela Press.

ISBN: 978-0-9995544-0-1

Butterflies, Dragonflies & Flowers
Adult Coloring Book

Mabela Press

Every day holds the possibility of a miracle.

Happiness is a butterfly, which when pursued, is always just beyond your grasp, but which, if you will sit down quietly, may alight upon you.

Nathaniel Hawthorne

The dragonfly brings dreams to reality and is the messenger of wisdom and enlightenment from other realms.

Author Unknown

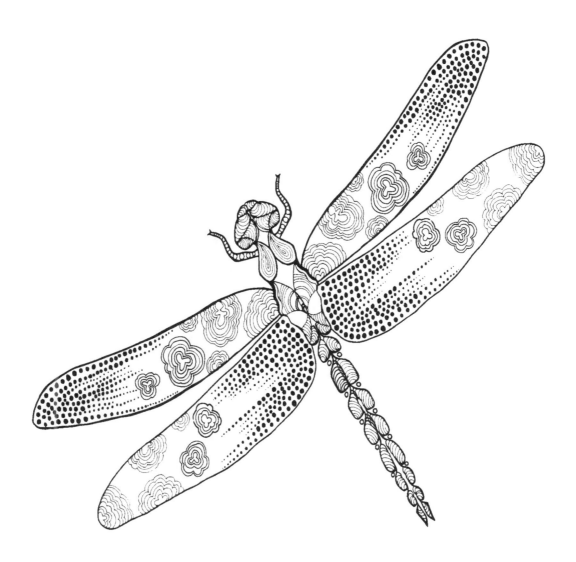

The foolish man seeks happiness in the distance;
the wise man grows it under his feet.

- James Oppenheim

Printed in the USA
CPSIA information can be obtained
at www.ICGtesting.com
LVHW080156151124
796706LV00010B/150